Our Galactic Community

A Keepsake Book of Fwendship and Love

Created by YOU!
(with help from Bayyo and Doccy)

This iS Me!

All About Me!

How I Found My Community

Fwendship is Love!

My First Fwends!

A Great Event!

Time to Party!!

A Time I Sent Wuv to a Fwend

A Time a Fwend Sent Wuv to Me

A Time I Cried

A Time I Laughed

I Will Always Remember...

ThiS iS US

This is Community

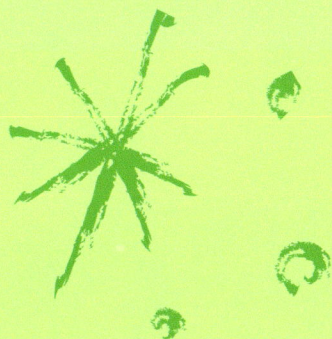

ThiS iS LoVe

More Memories

More Memories

Dedicated with Love
to All Our Fwends

Across the Galaxy
and Beyond

Ideas for How To Use this Book

Circles, lines, blank boxes, and other open spaces
are for you! These are the places you create your story!
You can leave the book as it is and create your story aloud,
by talking, or in your imagination all by yourself.
Or You Might Try...
Handwriting * Cutting and Pasting Typed Text * Photographs
* Drawings * Collage * Stickers *
Decorative tape * Postcards * Letters * Stamps *
Mementos * Personal Memories * Quotes * Lists * Poems *
And More!
Not Sure if a particular ink or adhesive will work on these
pages? Maybe test it in a small area of the More Memories
pages and give it time to dry to see.
Have fun!

Page-by-Page Ideas

First, whose book is this? Whatever your answer, that's the "you" for the rest of these tips. We are doing two books at our place: one for Doccy and one for Bayyo!

This is Me : You are a member of this community and you are important! Tell the world who you are! This page is designed for an image (pic or drawing) with a name, nickname, or screen name under it. But this is your book! Do whatever you want! Get as creative as you like! Maybe that arch is a window to another world?

All About Me : You can use pics, drawings, stickers, words, or whatever! Tell the world what you like, where you live, what you do, where you go...whatever makes you you.

How I Found My Community: Through words, images, or both, tell the story of how you found this wonderful galactic community!

My First Fwends and Fwendship is Love: Show or tell about your fwends in the community. Names, pictures, personalities, a signature style item, whatever lets us know who your fwends are. Stuck on this? Please keep reading.

A Great Event & Time to Party! These pages are to celebrate your celebrations, in person or virtual. If you were there, it counts! Maybe say or show the invitation, who attended, what you did, the theme, activities, a list of prompts, a scrap of wrapping paper or a party streamer? Whatever helps you remember the great gatherings!

Sending Wuv Pages - There are lots of ways to send wuv! Saying a prayer, sending a good thought, sending a message, an encouraging or supportive comment, a shoutout, a word of praise, attending someone's event, mentioning them in a speech or caption, tagging them in a social media post, sending or saying a thank you, happy mail, giving a gift, making them something, inviting them somewhere, drawing them a drawing, including them in something.
We bet you've sent lots of wuv and not even realized it!
Keep up the good work, fwends!

Bayyo would like to say something about receiving wuv: "Fwends, sometimes it feels like no one wuvs us or is our fwend. Dis happens to everyone, fwend. Here's what to do if you need help wif dis page. First, look at da list about sending wuv. Think back. Maybe there was one little time someone said or did something nice. That's when someone sent wuv to you."

"Bayyo still here, fwends. Always here.

If you still stuck on what to do for Fwendship or Wuv, please know dat Bayyo always loves you. Feel dat in your heart. Remember it whenever you want or need to. Even if I'm not there or can't always answer, Bayyo loves you."

We think you can figure out the rest of the pages on your own, fwends. But if you have questions, you're welcome to contact us!

Find us at:
Email: BayyoMail@gmail.com
Insta: @Dr.T_Writes
Fwenmail: PO Box 55, Palm Beach, FL 33480 USA
or one of our webpages
Enjoy the Book, Fwends!

Created by
BayYo and Doccy

+

You!

www.ingramcontent.com/pod-product-compliance
Lightning Source LLC
Chambersburg PA
CBHW040805300326

41914CB00064B/1607